A Guide to Having a Successful and Happy Home and Family Life

John E. Knopp Jr.

A Guide to Having a Successful and Happy Home and Family Life
John E. Knopp Jr.

Published By Parables
November, 2018

All Rights Reserved. No part of this book may be reproduced or utilized in any form or by any means, electronic or mechanical, including photocopying, recording, or by any information storage and retrieval system, without permission in writing from the author.

    ISBN 978-1-945698-90-3
    Printed in the United States of America

Readers should be aware that Internet Web sites offered as citations and/or sources for further information may have been changed or disappeared between the time this was written and the time it is read.

A Guide to Having a Successful and Happy Home and Family Life

John E. Knopp Jr.

Index

Chapter One: Priorities
1

Chapter Two: Family
35

Chapter Three: Career, Job, or Education.
47

Chapter Four: Study, Sharing, Helping others.
55

A Guide to Having a Successful and Happy Home and Family Life

Chapter One – Priorities

In life we often prioritize our lives, such as; schedules, friendships, needs, and desires.

Prioritizing if done in the proper sequences can be a very good way of having a good structured, calm, and happy life. Let's look at a few ways of prioritizing our lives.

Let us first take a look at how a Social Worker, Psychologist, or Secular Counselor might try to prioritize things:

Priority #1: Self must be put first and foremost above and before everything else. After all, if you don't take of yourself, and watch out for your own needs, who else can you expect to look after you? Also, if you don't look out for number one, (You are number One) how could you possibly be able to take care of anyone else?

Priority #2: Job or Career, (Go to school and get a degree in something if you are able) must be next. If you don't have an income, how can you support yourself and take care of yourself, and be able to say "I did it on my own"? After all shouldn't you be responsible for making and paying for your own way?

Priority #3: Your next priority must be to store up as much as you can for future use. You may want to retire comfortably or be able to make purchases, or possibly start a family at some later point in life.

Priority #4: OK, You now have a good career, a good nest egg for your future, make sure you take time for entertainment, relaxation, and fun. After all, too much work, and not enough play, makes Johnny a dull boy, maybe even boring.

Priority #5: Now, after much needed rest, you have all you need to be self sufficient, and will be able to live comfortably sometime in the future. Now you are ready to start a family. To find the right mate for yourself, you might use the following guide lines:

> **Rule #1**: Make sure you find someone that is very good to look at, after all, you may end up looking at them across the breakfast table, (at least for next couple of years anyways, until you realize that you cannot tolerate each other's petty annoyances any longer).
> **Rule #2**: Make sure your new (possible) life partner is successful and is able to fulfill all your personal needs, wants, and desires.

Rule #3: Make sure you and your new (possible) life partner agree on what you both want out of life.

Rule #4: Make sure your partner realizes that they need you more than you need them. (*You are only with this person because you choose to be.*)

Rule #5: It is ok for your partner to disagree with you, (*as long as you say it is ok, and it doesn't interfere with your life, happiness, and / or desires*).

Rule #6: If you have too many problems in your relationship, get rid of your partner, and start over with **Rule #1**.

Rule #7: If during this relationship, you are blessed with having children, and you decide to make a parting of the ways, do not use the children as pawns to get what you want, but only to get what you deserve, (*As seen only by your side of things, after all, it's your thoughts that matter most anyhow*).

Priority #6: Your children should come next, (*This is also a good way of getting even with your partner not doing it your way*). Make sure your children's needs are met, and that they have what is necessary, after all your needs, wants, and desires are met. (*Non-Essentials may be given or withheld in order to keep the children in line with your happiness, or used as a way to make your ex mate miserable*).

Priority #7: After everything else as noted in the previous priorities are met, you may wish to donate to some sort of charity to make you feel good. This is also a good way to impress others.

Now let's see how a Religious person (Not necessarily Christian) might think to prioritize things:

Priority #1: Church must be first and foremost above and before all other things in life, (*as long as it doesn't interfere with your general happiness, needs, or desires*).

> **Rule #1**: Everything that others might be able to see or hear about you or your family must be done to improve your social status in your local Church.
> **Rule #2**: If it is done behind closed doors, no-one else can see or hear about it, is ok, what others do not know is none of their business.

Priority #2: Your family must come next. If you can't take care of your family, how can you take care of the Lord's Sheep? Your family's needs, desires, and wants should be met before anything else. Also, remember, you are the head of your family, therefore your needs need to be met first in order for you to meet your family's needs.

Priority #3: Your Career, Job, or Education must come next. (*We should not expect God to meet all of our petty* *needs, wants, and desires. He has more important things to do. God helps those that help themselves.)*

Priority #4: Entertainment, relaxation, and fun, after everything else is done. Why should I not be able to relax and enjoy my life?

Now let's look how a Christian should prioritize things:

Priority #1: God, (Not necessarily the Church) should be your number one priority.

> **Rule #1**: Start and End each day with a prayer of Thanksgiving and a desire to know His Will and Desires for your life. Seek out His Will and Direction in order to Serve Him because He Loves you.
>
>> **A**: Prayer is a two way dialog in communication with our Lord. We must be able to hear His Voice as we seek out His Will, as well as speaking our petition of thanks giving and needs to Him.
>
> **Rule #2**: Give back to the Lord out of the best of the Blessings He allows you to receive with a cheerful heart.

Priority #2: Take care of the needs of your family.

Rule #1: Your partner in marriage should be put first inline after the Lord.

Rule #2: Your children should be put next in line after your partner, your partner is your life long help mate.

Rule #3: When you make yourself last in your priorities, the Lord will meet all of your needs, and your life will be made to be Blessed.

Priority #3: Your Career, Job, or Education should be next in order that you are able to take care of what the Lord has Blessed you with. (*This will also give you opportunities to Serve Him by the Witness of your actions and or words.*)

Priority #4: Out of the abundance of the Blessings that you receive from the Lord, seek out, and help others. (*Service to others' needs is a Service to the Lord, when done with a cheerful heart and desire to share your Richness of Blessings, as this may bring others to seek out the Lord.*)

As you can see, there are many different ideas on how to prioritize life.

How do you prioritize your life?

Do you seek out the Will of the Lord in all that you do?

Do you look for guidance from the Lord in which might be the best way to handle each situation that you might find yourself in?

God has given us His Word that we might know how to do things His way.

The only way to find out what His way is; is to dig in, read, study, and absorb His Words into the deepest part of our souls.

There are a good many people out there that "know" what the Bible says, however, they do not "understand" the meaning of what they "know".

Many believe that it is up to each person to interpret the Word as it applies to their situation, and that the Word can be made to fit whatever interpretation of meaning that allows them to legally fit their own way of thinking that best suits their needs or desires.

They might take sequences of Scripture out of context to make it fit into their way instead of conforming to God's way, which never changes.

We must study the whole Word of God that we might make ourselves approved, and through the study of the Word we can know what we are expected to do.

We can look at the Word as being our "Life's Instructions Manual".

If you want to know how to build a house, you might read a blue print that gives you the instructions on how to build the house. Do you believe that it is possible to build a house if five people are working on the same house, reading the same blue prints, but each has their own way interpreting the blue prints? What kind of house do you suppose might be made under this type of circumstance? Don't you think that five different interpretations of the same blue prints would cause some confusion?

The same applies to God's Word. The Word of God can only be interpreted One way, God's way, God is, was, and always will be, the same. His ways do not change because culture might change. The Bible interprets Itself within the pages of Itself. The Righteous Ways of God do not change to conform to the change in the culture of how man might look at things. If God said it is a sin then it is a sin. The Moral Character of God is an unmovable pillar.

In our society today, too many believe that morality is relative, if Society can agree that it is good; then it must be good. It is this very way of thinking that caused the destruction of Sodom and Gomorra. If we truly want to know what right, and what God's way is of doing things is, then we must give priority to Him and His Word, and study it, and make it a vital part of our lives, and our lifestyles.

Let's now take a look at some Scriptures that show how to prioritize our lives.

In the Book of Exodus, Chapter 20, God gives direct information on Who should be first in Priority;

Exo 20:1 And God spake all these words, saying,

Exo 20:2 I am the LORD thy God, which have brought thee out of the land of Egypt, out of the house of bondage.

Exo 20:3 Thou shalt have no other gods before me.

Exo 20:4 Thou shalt not make unto thee any graven image, or any likeness of anything that is in heaven above, or that is in the earth beneath, or that is in the water under the earth:

Exo 20:5 Thou shalt not bow down thyself to them, nor serve them: for I the LORD thy God am a jealous God, visiting the iniquity of the fathers upon the children unto the third and fourth generation of them that hate me;

Exo 20:6 And shewing mercy unto thousands of them that love me, and keep my commandments.

Exo 20:7 Thou shalt not take the name of the LORD thy God in vain; for the LORD will not hold him guiltless that taketh his name in vain.

In these Commands, Given to the Hebrew Children through Moses and From God, clearly shows that we are to put God First and foremost in our list of priorities.

Jesus tells us that God should be first in our lives in the Gospel of Matthew Chapter 22;

> *Mat 22:34 But when the Pharisees had heard that he had put the Sadducees to silence, they were gathered together.*
> *Mat 22:35 Then one of them, which was a lawyer, asked him a question, tempting him, and saying,*
> *Mat 22:36 Master, which is the great commandment in the law?*
> *Mat 22:37 Jesus said unto him, Thou shalt love the Lord thy God with all thy heart, and with all thy soul, and with all thy mind.*
> *Mat 22:38 This is the first and great commandment.*
> *Mat 22:39 And the second is like unto it, Thou shalt love thy neighbour as thyself.*
> *Mat 22:40 On these two commandments hang all the law and the prophets.*

Again we are told in Luke Chapter 12;

> *Luk 12:22 And he said unto his disciples, Therefore I say unto you, Take no thought for your life, what ye shall eat; neither for the body, what ye shall put on.*
> *Luk 12:23 The life is more than meat, and the body is more than raiment.*
> *Luk 12:24 Consider the ravens: for they neither sow nor reap; which neither have storehouse nor barn; and God feedeth them: how much more are ye better than the fowls?*

Luk 12:25 And which of you with taking thought can add to his stature one cubit?

Luk 12:26 If ye then be not able to do that thing which is least, why take ye thought for the rest?

Luk 12:27 Consider the lilies how they grow: they toil not, they spin not; and yet I say unto you, that Solomon in all his glory was not arrayed like one of these.

Luk 12:28 If then God so clothe the grass, which is to day in the field, and tomorrow is cast into the oven; how much more will he clothe you, O ye of little faith?

Luk 12:29 And seek not ye what ye shall eat, or what ye shall drink, neither be ye of doubtful mind.

Luk 12:30 For all these things do the nations of the world seek after: and your Father knoweth that ye have need of these things.

Luk 12:31 But rather seek ye the kingdom of God; and all these things shall be added unto you.

Luk 12:32 Fear not, little flock; for it is your Father's good pleasure to give you the kingdom.

Luk 12:33 Sell that ye have, and give alms; provide yourselves bags which wax not old, a treasure in the heavens that faileth not, where no thief approacheth, neither moth corrupteth.

Luk 12:34 For where your treasure is, there will your heart be also.

Jesus tells us that we cannot serve two masters, and that we are to first seek the kingdom of God, and then everything else would be added to us in the Gospel of John, Chapter 6;

Mat 6:18 That thou appear not unto men to fast, but unto thy Father which is in secret: and thy Father, which seeth in secret, shall reward thee openly.

Mat 6:19 Lay not up for yourselves treasures upon earth, where moth and rust doth corrupt, and where thieves break through and steal:

Mat 6:20 But lay up for yourselves treasures in heaven, where neither moth nor rust doth corrupt, and where thieves do not break through nor steal:

Mat 6:21 For where your treasure is, there will your heart be also.

Mat 6:22 The light of the body is the eye: if therefore thine eye be single, thy whole body shall be full of light.

Mat 6:23 But if thine eye be evil, thy whole body shall be full of darkness. If therefore the light that is in thee be darkness, how great is that darkness!

Mat 6:24 No man can serve two masters: for either he will hate the one, and love the other; or else he will hold to the one, and despise the other. Ye cannot serve God and mammon.

Mat 6:25 Therefore I say unto you, Take no thought for your life, what ye shall eat, or what ye shall drink; nor yet for your body, what ye shall put on. Is not the life more than meat, and the body than raiment?

Mat 6:26 Behold the fowls of the air: for they sow not, neither do they reap, nor gather into barns; yet your heavenly Father feedeth them. Are ye not much better than they?

> *Mat 6:27 Which of you by taking thought can add one cubit unto his stature?*
>
> *Mat 6:28 And why take ye thought for raiment? Consider the lilies of the field, how they grow; they toil not, neither do they spin:*
>
> *Mat 6:29 And yet I say unto you, That even Solomon in all his glory was not arrayed like one of these.*
>
> *Mat 6:30 Wherefore, if God so clothe the grass of the field, which today is, and tomorrow is cast into the oven, shall he not much more clothe you, O ye of little faith?*
>
> *Mat 6:31 Therefore take no thought, saying, What shall we eat? or, What shall we drink? or, Wherewithal shall we be clothed?*
>
> *Mat 6:32 (For after all these things do the Gentiles seek:) for your heavenly Father knoweth that ye have need of all these things.*
>
> *Mat 6:33 But seek ye first the kingdom of God, and his righteousness; and all these things shall be added unto you.*
>
> *Mat 6:34 Take therefore no thought for the morrow: for the morrow shall take thought for the things of itself. Sufficient unto the day is the evil thereof.*

So we see, Jesus gives us the example of putting God first in our order of priorities. When we look to Him for guidance and direction first, and then follow in His Service, I believe that our lives tend to be a whole lot less complicated, than it is when we just go off and do things our own way. We may get the job done our way, however when we follow His way, we tend to not only get the job done, but because we follow His direction and guidance, maybe along the way, we may be used as a vessel for leading others to Him that they also might come to know the joy that comes from His service.

Our thoughts ought to always begin with seeking out God's help in order that we might have a clean conscious in and out of our actions because we know that we are doing and giving our best first to the Lord, with whom nothing is impossible when God is involved in our decisions and directing our actions for His Divine purpose, that He can receive all the praise in the end.

When we put the Lord first, then we must be able to: Do (Our Actions allowing the Spirit to work through us; Our actions should reflect that of the Lord.), Go (If the Lord says go to Nineveh; we should not have to wait to be swallowed by a whale before doing what we are guided to do.), and Lead others into His flock.

This is how Jesus explained what we are to do when we are guided this way in the Gospel of Matthew Chapter 8;

> *Mat 8:18 Now when Jesus saw great multitudes about him, he gave commandment to depart unto the other side.*
> *Mat 8:19 And a certain scribe came, and said unto him, Master, I will follow thee whithersoever thou goest.*
> *Mat 8:20 And Jesus saith unto him, The foxes have holes, and the birds of the air have nests; but the Son of man hath not where to lay his head.*

> *Mat 8:21 And another of his disciples said unto him, Lord, suffer me first to go and bury my father.*
> *Mat 8:22 But Jesus said unto him, Follow me; and let the dead bury their dead.*

So as we can plainly see from the above Scriptures, When we hear God's instructions, we ought to get up and immediately do that which we are called to do.

Our actions will clearly define who we are, and who we belong to. The contents of our hearts will be proved in our actions.

Jesus tells us this in the Gospel of Matthew Chapter 12;

> *Mat 12:33 Either make the tree good, and his fruit good; or else make the tree corrupt, and his fruit corrupt: for the tree is known by his fruit.*
> *Mat 12:34 O generation of vipers, how can ye, being evil, speak good things? for out of the abundance of the heart the mouth speaketh.*
> *Mat 12:35 A good man out of the good treasure of the heart bringeth forth good things: and an evil man out of the evil treasure bringeth forth evil things.*
> *Mat 12:36 But I say unto you, That every idle word that men shall speak, they shall give account thereof in the day of judgment.*

Mat 12:37 For by thy words thou shalt be justified, and by thy words thou shalt be condemned.

The next priority in the life of the Christian family should be one's spouse.

Jesus explains this to us in the Gospel of Matthew Chapter 19;

Mat 19:3 The Pharisees also came unto him, tempting him, and saying unto him, Is it lawful for a man to put away his wife for every cause?

Mat 19:4 And he answered and said unto them, Have ye not read, that he which made them at the beginning made them male and female,

Mat 19:5 And said, For this cause shall a man leave father and mother, and shall cleave to his wife: and they twain shall be one flesh?

Mat 19:6 Wherefore they are no more twain, but one flesh. What therefore God hath joined together, let not man put asunder.

Mat 19:7 They say unto him, Why did Moses then command to give a writing of divorcement, and to put her away?

Mat 19:8 He saith unto them, Moses because of the hardness of your hearts suffered you to put away your wives: but from the beginning it was not so.

Mat 19:9 And I say unto you, Whosoever shall put away his wife, except it be for fornication, and shall marry another, committeth adultery: and whoso marrieth her which is put away doth commit adultery.

Mat 19:10 His disciples say unto him, If the case of the man be so with his wife, it is not good to marry.

In the Book of Ephesians Chapter 5, we are given an outline of how the Order of Command should be in a Christian home;

Eph 5:1 Be ye therefore followers of God, as dear children;

Eph 5:2 And walk in love, as Christ also hath loved us, and hath given himself for us an offering and a sacrifice to God for a sweet smelling savour.

Eph 5:3 But fornication, and all uncleanness, or covetousness, let it not be once named among you, as becometh saints;

Eph 5:4 Neither filthiness, nor foolish talking, nor jesting, which are not convenient: but rather giving of thanks.

Eph 5:5 For this ye know, that no whoremonger, nor unclean person, nor covetous man, who is an idolater, hath any inheritance in the kingdom of Christ and of God.

Eph 5:6 Let no man deceive you with vain words: for because of these things cometh the wrath of God upon the children of disobedience.

Eph 5:7 Be not ye therefore partakers with them.

Eph 5:8 For ye were sometimes darkness, but now are ye light in the Lord: walk as children of light:

Eph 5:9 (For the fruit of the Spirit is in all goodness and righteousness and truth;)

Eph 5:10 Proving what is acceptable unto the Lord.

Eph 5:11 And have no fellowship with the unfruitful works of darkness, but rather reprove them.

Eph 5:12 For it is a shame even to speak of those things which are done of them in secret.

Eph 5:13 But all things that are reproved are made manifest by the light: for whatsoever doth make manifest is light.

Eph 5:14 Wherefore he saith, Awake thou that sleepest, and arise from the dead, and Christ shall give thee light.

Eph 5:15 See then that ye walk circumspectly, not as fools, but as wise,

Eph 5:16 Redeeming the time, because the days are evil.

Eph 5:17 Wherefore be ye not unwise, but understanding what the will of the Lord is.

Eph 5:18 And be not drunk with wine, wherein is excess; but be filled with the Spirit;

Eph 5:19 Speaking to yourselves in psalms and hymns and spiritual songs, singing and making melody in your heart to the Lord;

Eph 5:20 Giving thanks always for all things unto God and the Father in the name of our Lord Jesus Christ;

Eph 5:21 Submitting yourselves one to another in the fear of God.

Eph 5:22 Wives, submit yourselves unto your own husbands, as unto the Lord.

Eph 5:23 For the husband is the head of the wife, even as Christ is the head of the church: and he is the saviour of the body.

Eph 5:24 Therefore as the church is subject unto Christ, so let the wives be to their own husbands in everything.

Eph 5:25 Husbands, love your wives, even as Christ also loved the church, and gave himself for it;

Eph 5:26 That he might sanctify and cleanse it with the washing of water by the word,

Eph 5:27 That he might present it to himself a glorious church, not having spot, or wrinkle, or any such thing; but that it should be holy and without blemish.

Eph 5:28 So ought men to love their wives as their own bodies. He that loveth his wife loveth himself.

Eph 5:29 For no man ever yet hated his own flesh; but nourisheth and cherisheth it, even as the Lord the church:

Eph 5:30 For we are members of his body, of his flesh, and of his bones.

Eph 5:31 For this cause shall a man leave his father and mother, and shall be joined unto his wife, and they two shall be one flesh.

Eph 5:32 This is a great mystery: but I speak concerning Christ and the church.

> *Eph 5:33 Nevertheless let every one of you in particular so love his wife even as himself; and the wife see that she reverence her husband.*

So, you see, we are to put Christ as the Head of All life; He is the only begotten Son of God, He alone came to Earth to take our place in Spiritual Death on the Cross, in order that we be able to be reconciled back to God. *(If we then follow Christ's teachings, then one should note that when one is made to be the head [as Christ is the Head of the Church], then we should understand that the best way to be the head, is to also follow Christ's example of being the head [FIRST]through serving those under us in our own actions;*

(Just as Jesus taught us in the Gospel of Luke 22:24-30)

> *Luke 22:24 And there was also a strife among them, which of them should be accounted the greatest.*
> *Luke 22:25 And he said unto them, The kings of the Gentiles exercise lordship over them; and they that exercise authority upon them are called benefactors.*
> *Luke 22:26 But ye shall not be so: but he that is greatest among you, let him be as the younger; and he that is chief, as he that doth serve.*
> *Luke 22:27 For whether is greater, he that sitteth at meat, or he that serveth? is not he that sitteth at meat? but I am among you as he that serveth.*

> *Luke 22:28 Ye are they which have continued with me in my temptations.*
> *Luke 22:29 And I appoint unto you a kingdom, as my Father hath appointed unto me;*
> *Luke 22:30 That ye may eat and drink at my table in my kingdom, and sit on thrones judging the twelve tribes of Israel.*

After Christ, the Husband is the Head of the home, (He should be teaching by Godly example, to his family that which is correct and moral, that the family should follow his steps and put the Lord first.) Next in line, the Husband should put the Wife as is next priority, (Please re-read Ephesians 5:28-33.) and the Husband and Wife should be as one flesh, (Working together as Partners, not One in control of the other, thereby making each other Whole, able to be best suited to serve the Lord.

Your children should be the next in line on your list of priorities,

as Ephesians Chapter 6 tells us;

> *Eph 6:1 Children, obey your parents in the Lord: for this is right.*
> *Eph 6:2 Honour thy father and mother; (which is the first commandment with promise;)*
> *Eph 6:3 That it may be well with thee, and thou mayest live long on the earth.*

Eph 6:4 And, ye fathers, provoke not your children to wrath: but bring them up in the nurture and admonition of the Lord.

As Christians, we should raise up our Children in the ways of the Lord in order that they shall be prepared to live a life of servitude to the Lord.

Proverbs Chapter 22 tells us;

> *Pro 22:3 A prudent man foreseeth the evil, and hideth himself: but the simple pass on, and are punished.*
> *Pro 22:4 By humility and the fear of the LORD are riches, and honour, and life.*
> *Pro 22:5 Thorns and snares are in the way of the froward: he that doth keep his soul shall be far from them.*
> *Pro 22:6 Train up a child in the way he should go: and when he is old, he will not depart from it.*
> *Pro 22:7 The rich ruleth over the poor, and the borrower is servant to the lender.*
> *Pro 22:8 He that soweth iniquity shall reap vanity: and the rod of his anger shall fail.*
> *Pro 22:9 He that hath a bountiful eye shall be blessed; for he giveth of his bread to the poor.*
> *Pro 22:10 Cast out the scorner, and contention shall go out; yea, strife and reproach shall cease.*
> *Pro 22:11 He that loveth pureness of heart, for the grace of his lips the king shall be his friend.*

Pro 22:12 The eyes of the LORD preserve knowledge, and he over throweth the words of the transgressor.

Pro 22:13 The slothful man saith, There is a lion without, I shall be slain in the streets.

Pro 22:14 The mouth of strange women is a deep pit: he that is abhorred of the LORD shall fall therein.

Pro 22:15 Foolishness is bound in the heart of a child; but the rod of correction shall drive it far from him.

If we train our children up together (Mother and Father / Husband and Wife) by teaching what is right in the sight of the Lord, by our living examples, We will be teaching our children how to serve the Lord out of Love, and not just because "the Bible says so". We should look upon our becoming Parents as a Gift; children should be considered as gifts, to be cherished and taken care of. (Children should not be looked upon as being owned as a possession, but as a Soul that is temporarily loaned to us, that we might bring them up in the ways of the Lord.) Children should be cherished and considered among our most valued assets. An example to this statement would be such as; if you lived on a farm, and you have some type of livestock on your farm, would you not count the livestock as valuable assets? Of course, you would. You would raise your livestock up to bring you the best very value possible. Children should be raised up in the same way, to be valuable assets for the Lord. When we interact with our children positively, we teach them positive values such as;

1. They are valuable because we take the time to spend with them, talk with them, (***NOTE**: *talk with; not to*), and we teach them positive moral values, and the difference between right from wrong(It is our duty as Christian Parents to bring our children up in the ways of the Lord).

2. They are important because we take the time to; listen to what they have to say, how they feel.

3. We teach our children how to respect others by showing them respect in the way we deal with them, in speech and actions.

4. We show them that they have value because we care enough to show them discipline when they are disobedient.

Proverbs Chapter 3, Verses 11,12 tells us;
> *Pro 3:11 My son, despise not the chastening of the LORD; neither be weary of his correction:*
> *Pro 3:12 For whom the LORD loveth he correcteth; even as a father the son in whom he delighteth.)*

Our next priority as Christians should be to teach our children the value of supporting your family.

When Parents teach their children the value of a day's labor, and how to do everything as if it is in direct service to the Lord, (Do everything to the best of your ability), our children learn moral values, and that giving their best gives everyone a sense of well being that also gives glory back to God.

Colossians Chapter 3 Verse 17 tells us;

Col 3:17 And whatsoever ye do in word or deed, do all in the name of the Lord Jesus, giving thanks to God and the Father by him.

Ephesians Chapter 4 Verse 28 tells us;

Eph 4:28 Let him that stole steal no more: but rather let him labour, working with his hands the thing which is good, that he may have to give to him that needeth.

Ecclesiastes Chapter 3 tells us;

Ecc 3:1 To every thing there is a season, and a time to every purpose under the heaven:
Ecc 3:2 A time to be born, and a time to die; a time to plant, and a time to pluck up that which is planted;
Ecc 3:3 A time to kill, and a time to heal; a time to break down, and a time to build up;
Ecc 3:4 A time to weep, and a time to laugh; a time to mourn, and a time to dance;
Ecc 3:5 A time to cast away stones, and a time to gather stones together; a time to embrace, and a time to refrain from embracing;

Ecc 3:6 A time to get, and a time to lose; a time to keep, and a time to cast away;

Ecc 3:7 A time to rend, and a time to sew; a time to keep silence, and a time to speak;

Ecc 3:8 A time to love, and a time to hate; a time of war, and a time of peace.

Ecc 3:9 What profit hath he that worketh in that wherein he laboureth?

Ecc 3:10 I have seen the travail, which God hath given to the sons of men to be exercised in it.

Ecc 3:11 He hath made every thing beautiful in his time: also he hath set the world in their heart, so that no man can find out the work that God maketh from the beginning to the end.

Ecc 3:12 I know that there is no good in them, but for a man to rejoice, and to do good in his life.

Ecc 3:13 And also that every man should eat and drink, and enjoy the good of all his labour, it is the gift of God.

Remember; Children learn more from what they see than that which they only hear about. When we set the example that we want our children, and or grandchildren to learn by living it ourselves, (As parents), then we are teaching them by our example, just as Jesus said, "I know only what I have seen of my Father", our children will learn the same Christian, (or not Christian) values as we live them ourselves. Too many people today have the {Do what I tell you, not as I do} mentality, and then expect others to do what is right without any sort of real guidance.

A Guide to Having a Successful and Happy Home and Family Life

Psalms Chapter 1 tells us:
> *Psa 1:1 Blessed is the man that walketh not in the counsel of the ungodly, nor standeth in the way of sinners, nor sitteth in the seat of the scornful.*
> *Psa 1:2 But his delight is in the law of the LORD; and in his law doth he meditate day and night.*
> *Psa 1:3 And he shall be like a tree planted by the rivers of water, that bringeth forth his fruit in his season; his leaf also shall not wither; and whatsoever he doeth shall prosper.*
> *Psa 1:4 The ungodly are not so: but are like the chaff which the wind driveth away.*
> *Psa 1:5 Therefore the ungodly shall not stand in the judgment, nor sinners in the congregation of the righteous.*
> *Psa 1:6 For the LORD knoweth the way of the righteous: but the way of the ungodly shall perish.*

We must honor the Lord for the blessings that He shines upon us, (We are all blessed each and every day, and it is easy and plain to see if only we would open our hearts, minds, and eyes to see all that the Lord gives to us). We should give thanks for all things, acknowledging that it all comes from the Lord. We ought to be praising Him in our worship, in our speaking, and all our actions.

Psalms Chapter 17 tells us:

Psa 17:1 A Prayer of David. Hear the right, O LORD, attend unto my cry, give ear unto my prayer, that goeth not out of feigned lips.

Psa 17:2 Let my sentence come forth from thy presence; let thine eyes behold the things that are equal.

Psa 17:3 Thou hast proved mine heart; thou hast visited me in the night; thou hast tried me, and shalt find nothing; I am purposed that my mouth shall not transgress.

Psa 17:4 Concerning the works of men, by the word of thy lips I have kept me from the paths of the destroyer.

Psa 17:5 Hold up my goings in thy paths, that my footsteps slip not.

Psa 17:6 I have called upon thee, for thou wilt hear me, O God: incline thine ear unto me, and hear my speech.

Psa 17:7 Shew thy marvellous lovingkindness, O thou that savest by thy right hand them which put their trust in thee from those that rise up against them.

Psa 17:8 Keep me as the apple of the eye, hide me under the shadow of thy wings,

Psa 17:9 From the wicked that oppress me, from my deadly enemies, who compass me about.

Psa 17:10 They are inclosed in their own fat: with their mouth they speak proudly.

Psa 17:11 They have now compassed us in our steps: they have set their eyes bowing down to the earth;

> *Psa 17:12 Like as a lion that is greedy of his prey, and as it were a young lion lurking in secret places.*
> *Psa 17:13 Arise, O LORD, disappoint him, cast him down: deliver my soul from the wicked, which is thy sword:*
> *Psa 17:14 From men which are thy hand, O LORD, from men of the world, which have their portion in this life, and whose belly thou fillest with thy hid treasure: they are full of children, and leave the rest of their substance to their babes.*
> *Psa 17:15 As for me, I will behold thy face in righteousness: I shall be satisfied, when I awake, with thy likeness.*

We should begin and end each and every day in communication with the Lord, asking Him for direction and guidance in order that we might do His Will, and serve Him in all that we do. Each day is a new opportunity to serve the Lord in order to lead others to Him. (Remember, communication only works when it is spoken and heard by two or more persons speaking and hearing each other).

It is only when we can understand that our lives can only be whole and complete when we seek out and follow the Lord; it is only then that we can truly understand the kind of Love that our Creator has for us, (His Creation). We love, because we see God's Love. Have you given your life over to the service of the Lord yet? Have you been set free from the bonds of sin by believing in and calling upon the Name of the Lord; Jesus, the One who died on the cross for you? The First Resurrected from the dead? His Blood covers the multitude of all our sins for those who believe. Brother or Sister, please seek Him out and accept Him, it is only in Him that you can be set free, and His yoke is light compared to that of this world. He is waiting, are you ready? His Word tells us that He will return for His Church, will you be waiting and ready? Are really certain that you have time to wait? His word tells us that He will come when He is not expected, as thief in the night, when no one is watching.

Matthew Chapter Twenty-Five tells us:

Mat 25:1 Then shall the kingdom of heaven be likened unto ten virgins, which took their lamps, and went forth to meet the bridegroom.
Mat 25:2 And five of them were wise, and five were foolish.
Mat 25:3 They that were foolish took their lamps, and took no oil with them:
Mat 25:4 But the wise took oil in their vessels with their lamps.
Mat 25:5 While the bridegroom tarried, they all slumbered and slept.
Mat 25:6 And at midnight there was a cry made, Behold, the bridegroom cometh; go ye out to meet him.
Mat 25:7 Then all those virgins arose, and trimmed their lamps.
Mat 25:8 And the foolish said unto the wise, Give us of your oil; for our lamps are gone out.

Mat 25:9 But the wise answered, saying, Not so; lest there be not enough for us and you: but go ye rather to them that sell, and buy for yourselves.

Mat 25:10 And while they went to buy, the bridegroom came; and they that were ready went in with him to the marriage: and the door was shut.

Mat 25:11 Afterward came also the other virgins, saying, Lord, Lord, open to us.

Mat 25:12 But he answered and said, Verily I say unto you, I know you not.

Mat 25:13 Watch therefore, for ye know neither the day nor the hour wherein the Son of man cometh.

Mat 25:14 For the kingdom of heaven is as a man travelling into a far country, who called his own servants, and delivered unto them his goods.

Mat 25:15 And unto one he gave five talents, to another two, and to another one; to every man according to his several ability; and straightway took his journey.

Mat 25:16 Then he that had received the five talents went and traded with the same, and made them other five talents.

Mat 25:17 And likewise he that had received two, he also gained other two.

Mat 25:18 But he that had received one went and digged in the earth, and hid his lord's money.

Mat 25:19 After a long time the lord of those servants cometh, and reckoneth with them.

Mat 25:20 And so he that had received five talents came and brought other five talents, saying, Lord, thou deliveredst unto me five talents: behold, I have gained beside them five talents more.

Mat 25:21 His lord said unto him, Well done, thou good and faithful servant: thou hast been faithful over a few things, I will make thee ruler over many things: enter thou into the joy of thy lord.

Mat 25:22 He also that had received two talents came and said, Lord, thou deliveredst unto me two talents: behold, I have gained two other talents beside them.

Mat 25:23 His lord said unto him, Well done, good and faithful servant; thou hast been faithful over a few things, I will make thee ruler over many things: enter thou into the joy of thy lord.

Mat 25:24 Then he which had received the one talent came and said, Lord, I knew thee that thou art an hard man, reaping where thou hast not sown, and gathering where thou hast not strawed:

Mat 25:25 And I was afraid, and went and hid thy talent in the earth: lo, there thou hast that is thine.

Mat 25:26 His lord answered and said unto him, Thou wicked and slothful servant, thou knewest that I reap where I sowed not, and gather where I have not strawed:

Mat 25:27 Thou oughtest therefore to have put my money to the exchangers, and then at my coming I should have received mine own with usury.

Mat 25:28 Take therefore the talent from him, and give it unto him which hath ten talents.

Mat 25:29 For unto every one that hath shall be given, and he shall have abundance: but from him that hath not shall be taken away even that which he hath.

Mat 25:30 And cast ye the unprofitable servant into outer darkness: there shall be weeping and gnashing of teeth.

Mat 25:31 When the Son of man shall come in his glory, and all the holy angels with him, then shall he sit upon the throne of his glory:

Mat 25:32 And before him shall be gathered all nations: and he shall separate them one from another, as a shepherd divideth his sheep from the goats:

Mat 25:33 And he shall set the sheep on his right hand, but the goats on the left.

Mat 25:34 Then shall the King say unto them on his right hand, Come, ye blessed of my Father, inherit the kingdom prepared for you from the foundation of the world:

Mat 25:35 For I was an hungred, and ye gave me meat: I was thirsty, and ye gave me drink: I was a stranger, and ye took me in:

Mat 25:36 Naked, and ye clothed me: I was sick, and ye visited me: I was in prison, and ye came unto me.

Mat 25:37 Then shall the righteous answer him, saying, Lord, when saw we thee an hungred, and fed thee? or thirsty, and gave thee drink?

Mat 25:38 When saw we thee a stranger, and took thee in? or naked, and clothed thee?

Mat 25:39 Or when saw we thee sick, or in prison, and came unto thee?

Mat 25:40 And the King shall answer and say unto them, Verily I say unto you, Inasmuch as ye have done it unto one of the least of these my brethren, ye have done it unto me.

Mat 25:41 Then shall he say also unto them on the left hand, Depart from me, ye cursed, into everlasting fire, prepared for the devil and his angels:

Mat 25:42 For I was an hungred, and ye gave me no meat: I was thirsty, and ye gave me no drink:

Mat 25:43 I was a stranger, and ye took me not in: naked, and ye clothed me not: sick, and in prison, and ye visited me not.

Mat 25:44 Then shall they also answer him, saying, Lord, when saw we thee an hungred, or athirst, or a stranger, or naked, or sick, or in prison, and did not minister unto thee?

Mat 25:45 Then shall he answer them, saying, Verily I say unto you, Inasmuch as ye did it not to one of the least of these, ye did it not to me.

Mat 25:46 And these shall go away into everlasting punishment: but the righteous into life eternal.

Chapter Two: Family

Let me start this chapter out with a question;
How important is your family to you?
Do you show your family how much you care?
Or do you just expect them to know?

Let's make a list of our family life;

1. Do you say I Love you, (*In words and Actions*)?
2. Does your family Worship the Lord together?
3. Do you Pray together?
4. Do you make or take the time to spend with your family, in order to show them your love, that you care about them, and to teach them about the Lord?
5. Do you take the time to <u>*Discipline*</u> your children; to teach them what is right in the Lord? Discipline should be used to teach right from wrong, and never as a way for you to get even with your loved one for being disobedient. Discipline teaches where abuse comes from the need to get even.

Let's see what the Bible teaches about Family:

It is God, our Creator that first instituted Marriage and Family as we see in the Scriptures, starting in Genesis Chapter 2 Verses 18 through 25.

> *Gen 2:18 And the LORD God said, It is not good that the man should be alone; I will make him an help meet for him.*
>
> *Gen 2:19 And out of the ground the LORD God formed every beast of the field, and every fowl of the air; and brought them unto Adam to see what he would call them: and whatsoever Adam called every living creature, that was the name thereof.*
>
> *Gen 2:20 And Adam gave names to all cattle, and to the fowl of the air, and to every beast of the field; but for Adam there was not found an help meet for him.*
>
> *Gen 2:21 And the LORD God caused a deep sleep to fall upon Adam, and he slept: and he took one of his ribs, and closed up the flesh instead thereof;*
>
> *Gen 2:22 And the rib, which the LORD God had taken from man, made he a woman, and brought her unto the man.*
>
> *Gen 2:23 And Adam said, This is now bone of my bones, and flesh of my flesh: she shall be called Woman, because she was taken out of Man.*
>
> *Gen 2:24 Therefore shall a man leave his father and his mother, and shall cleave unto his wife: and they shall be one flesh.*
>
> *Gen 2:25 And they were both naked, the man and his wife, and were not ashamed.*

Here we see that God gave us Marriage as a gift to us, that we might have a partner to be a helpmate to each other. It is in Marriage that each partner should take the responsibility for each other, taking care of each other as partners.

Some might attempt to use Biblical Scriptures, (<u>*taken out of context*</u>), as a means to bully their Spouse into submission to themselves, believing that men are superior to women, and as such, try to make the woman bow before him, and obey his every command or desire. If we really take a good hard, and closer look into what the Scripture really says; we will find men and women are equal to each other in rank.

God made Eve from a rib taken from Adam's side, that she might walk beside him as a helpmate and partner in life.

God did not make Eve from Adam's foot, that she should be his doormat, or stepping stool, or to be kicked around, and to hoard over her as one would make over a slave. God also did not make Eve from Adam's hand, that she should be made into his personal punching bag and to be abused.

God shows us His Wisdom in making Eve from Adam's rib in his side, teaching us about partnerships and relationships.

Take note to the structure in which God made man and woman.

1. God formed man from the dust and breathed into man's nostril the breath of life, thereby making him a living soul.
2. God made woman by using a part of the created man, that they should cleave together and be as one.

How does God show us that Creation is reproduced beyond the first Created man and woman?

1. Woman gives life to her offspring in Birth.

    A. You see, We as Created beings cannot remain without each other, man and woman.
    B. Man cannot reproduce without the eggs produced by the woman, and Women cannot reproduce without the fertilization of the man's seed.

God also gives us the Outline of what Marriage is, as well as the reason for its institution:

    A. One Man, One Woman, cleaving together and becoming as one.
    B. This One Woman and One Man, after joining themselves together and becoming as One Flesh, are to Reproduce offspring.

We are shown in Ephesians Chapter 5;

Just as Jesus is the Head of the Church, leading us by His example of Love, the Husband is the Head of the Wife, (Recognizing that it is his duty to: Be responsible for caring for his wife's needs, and to be her protector, and to Love her as Christ loves His Church).

Husbands, how many of you love your wife enough to give up your life in order to save her life? As husbands we should be willing, if necessary, to give up our lives for our wife, just as Jesus gave His life for His Church. And just the same as husbands submit to Christ in the Light of His Holy Love, Wives should submit to their Husbands in the same way, out of the light of the Husband's love for his wife.

When one puts themselves in submission to another in Love, they are giving honor to them.

We are all to Submit ourselves in Spirit to Christ, and in doing so we follow His Commands and Teachings as He Himself showed us in the way He taught His Disciples.

> *Eph 5:15 See then that ye walk circumspectly, not as fools, but as wise,*
> *Eph 5:16 Redeeming the time, because the days are evil.*
> *Eph 5:17 Wherefore be ye not unwise, but understanding what the will of the Lord is.*
> *Eph 5:18 And be not drunk with wine, wherein is excess; but be filled with the Spirit;*
> *Eph 5:19 Speaking to yourselves in psalms and hymns and spiritual songs, singing and making melody in your heart to the Lord;*

Eph 5:20 Giving thanks always for all things unto God and the Father in the name of our Lord Jesus Christ;

Eph 5:21 Submitting yourselves one to another in the fear of God.

Eph 5:22 Wives, submit yourselves unto your own husbands, as unto the Lord.

Eph 5:23 For the husband is the head of the wife, even as Christ is the head of the church: and he is the saviour of the body.

Eph 5:24 Therefore as the church is subject unto Christ, so let the wives be to their own husbands in everything.

Eph 5:25 Husbands, love your wives, even as Christ also loved the church, and gave himself for it;

Eph 5:26 That he might sanctify and cleanse it with the washing of water by the word,

Eph 5:27 That he might present it to himself a glorious church, not having spot, or wrinkle, or any such thing; but that it should be holy and without blemish.

Eph 5:28 So ought men to love their wives as their own bodies. He that loveth his wife loveth himself.

Eph 5:29 For no man ever yet hated his own flesh; but nourisheth and cherisheth it, even as the Lord the church:

Eph 5:30 For we are members of his body, of his flesh, and of his bones.

> *Eph 5:31 For this cause shall a man leave his father and mother, and shall be joined unto his wife, and they two shall be one flesh.*
> *Eph 5:32 This is a great mystery: but I speak concerning Christ and the church.*
> *Eph 5:33 Nevertheless let every one of you in particular so love his wife even as himself; and the wife see that she reverence her husband.*

Likewise, our children should submit to their parents; children should be taught to follow the instructions and teachings of their parents in order that they might find Wisdom in serving the Lord.

When Children do disobey, dishonor, or disrespect their parents; A parent that loves their child should Chastise (Discipline) that child out of Love, in order to Teach that child right from wrong, that they might Honor the Lord when they are grown.

Just as in Proverbs Chapter Three teaches that those that the Lord loves, He Chastises; As we love our children when they do wrong we should chastise:

> *Pro 3:11 My son, despise not the chastening of the LORD; neither be weary of his correction:*
> *Pro 3:12 For whom the LORD loveth he correcteth; even as a father the son in whom he delighteth.*
> *Pro 3:13 Happy is the man that findeth wisdom, and the man that getteth understanding.*

Proverbs Chapter 13 teaches us:
> Pro 13:24 He that spareth his rod hateth his son: but he that loveth him chasteneth him betimes.

Proverbs Chapter 19 teaches us:
> Pro 19:18 Chasten thy son while there is hope, and let not thy soul spare for his crying.

Proverbs Chapter 22 teaches us:
> Pro 22:15 Foolishness is bound in the heart of a child; but the rod of correction shall drive it far from him.

Proverbs Chapter 23 teaches us:
> Pro 23:12 Apply thine heart unto instruction, and thine ears to the words of knowledge.
>
> Pro 23:13 Withhold not correction from the child: for if thou beatest him with the rod, he shall not die.
>
> Pro 23:14 Thou shalt beat him with the rod, and shalt deliver his soul from hell.
>
> Pro 23:15 My son, if thine heart be wise, my heart shall rejoice, even mine.
>
> Pro 23:16 Yea, my reins shall rejoice, when thy lips speak right things.

Proverbs Chapter 29 teaches us:
> Pro 29:15 The rod and reproof give wisdom: but a child left to himself bringeth his mother to shame.
>
> Pro 29:16 When the wicked are multiplied, transgression increaseth: but the righteous shall see their fall.

> *Pro 29:17 Correct thy son, and he shall give thee rest; yea, he shall give delight unto thy soul.*
> *Pro 29:18 Where there is no vision, the people perish: but he that keepeth the law, happy is he.*
> *Pro 29:19 A servant will not be corrected by words: for though he understand he will not answer.*

Parents, if you love your children, teach them the ways of the Word, and when they disobey, discipline them in love that they might learn wisdom and in turn follow the righteous ways of the Lord.

Take time to spend with your children, teach them by your example how they ought to be, after all; if our children do not see our example, who's example are they seeing, and in turn emulating?

Husbands, make time for your wives, that they might know that you love them by your example to them.

Wives, make time for your husbands that they might cover you with their love, and that by your example also teach Wisdom to your children on the true love that comes only from God.

Worship together daily, in prayer and study and teach the Word, that you may be ready at the appointed time when the Lord calls upon you. (If you don't take the time to teach the Holy Word, don't expect that anyone else will either. Remember; Children will learn what the live, and actions teach better than words. What do you wish for your family to learn?

When families study and pray together, and worship together giving praise unto the Lord, The family tends to stay together, are happier with less material objects, and satisfied with all their needs being met in the presence of the Lord.

Parents teach your children the importance of providing for your family, and that they should not expect to be entitled to what others have worked for, instead of providing for themselves.

The worldly way of doing things today teaches that everyone is entitled to receive free benefits that they have not themselves earned. The world's idea of spreading the wealth is not Biblical. The Bible teaches that one should provide for one's family through their labor. If one is able, then they should be taught necessary skills to provide for themselves.

We should however be willing to give a hand up, instead of giving hand outs.
If we give a man a fish, he can eat for a day, if we teach that man how to fish, he can now eat every day, (*I do not remember who coined this phrase, but it fits in all manners of life*).

We need to teach our family's to give back unto the Lord a portion of what He allows us to receive. When the Lord blesses us, we should in turn show our appreciation and give back a portion from the best of the best. When you practice this as a whole family, your whole family will be greatly blessed, and others that are watching you may come to want to know the Lord that is giving you these blessings.

To give back to the LORD His portion includes more than money that you put into the offering plate when / if you put into the plate when in a church service. The LORD has given each of us gifts of the Spirit to enable us to work in His service. What kind of gift(s) might you have? Can you sing? Can you teach? Can you cook? Anything that you might be able to do to help, teach, or show someone even a glimpse of the Lord is a gift. How are you taking care of the gift(s) the Lord has given to you? Are you being a good steward with your gift(s)?

John E. Knopp Jr.

Chapter Three:
Career, Job, or Education

We must remember; whatever we might be doing, all that we have is a blessing from GOD.

All things are under GOD's control, even when sometimes it may seem that evil is all abound, in the end we will all be judged according to our actions and how we behaved in our service or refusal to serve in all that we do or say.

1. If you are an employee of someone;
    A. Do all things as if you are doing them in service directly unto the LORD.
    B. Do your best without complaint remembering, (*at least you have employment, I'm certain that there is someone out there that would be happy to do your job because they may have lost their job due to the*

economy, lack of skills, or any number of reasons that they might be unemployed), you will be repaid for your service at the end when all will be judged.

C. Be thankful that the LORD has seen fit to give you the opportunity to serve HIM using whatever gift(s) that you might have.

2. If you are an employer;

    A. Be fair to all of those that you employ.

    B. If you employ one that has a need of training, do not be lacking as those that you train, may turn out to be your best workers.

    C. Maintain your Christian character and morality in order that through you, a greater Harvest may be Planted unto the Lord.

3. If you are self-employed;

    A. Be a good Steward of the gift(s) that you were given from the LORD, that you might do your very best in all that you do in order that the LORD shall receive honor.

4. Do all things that you do in order to bring glory unto the Lord. When you give claim to being a Christian, if you give or do anything other than your best, those who are watching you may be turned away from coming to and / or accepting Christ as their Lord and Savior, with you becoming a stumbling block.

We are taught in the Book of Proverbs:
Proverbs Chapter 3 verses 1-10;

Pro 3:1 My son, forget not my law; but let thine heart keep my commandments:

Pro 3:2 For length of days, and long life, and peace, shall they add to thee.

Pro 3:3 Let not mercy and truth forsake thee: bind them about thy neck; write them upon the table of thine heart:

Pro 3:4 So shalt thou find favour and good understanding in the sight of God and man.

Pro 3:5 Trust in the LORD with all thine heart; and lean not unto thine own understanding.

Pro 3:6 In all thy ways acknowledge him, and he shall direct thy paths.

Pro 3:7 Be not wise in thine own eyes: fear the LORD, and depart from evil.

Pro 3:8 It shall be health to thy navel, and marrow to thy bones.

Pro 3:9 Honour the LORD with thy substance, and with the firstfruits of all thine increase:

Pro 3:10 So shall thy barns be filled with plenty, and thy presses shall burst out with new wine.

Proverbs Chapter 3 verses 25 – 35 Teaches us:

Pro 3:25 Be not afraid of sudden fear, neither of the desolation of the wicked, when it cometh.

Pro 3:26 For the LORD shall be thy confidence, and shall keep thy foot from being taken.

Pro 3:27 Withhold not good from them to whom it is due, when it is in the power of thine hand to do it.

Pro 3:28 Say not unto thy neighbour, Go, and come again, and to morrow I will give; when thou hast it by thee.

Pro 3:29 Devise not evil against thy neighbour, seeing he dwelleth securely by thee.

Pro 3:30 Strive not with a man without cause, if he have done thee no harm.

Pro 3:31 Envy thou not the oppressor, and choose none of his ways.

Pro 3:32 For the froward is abomination to the LORD: but his secret is with the righteous.

Pro 3:33 The curse of the LORD is in the house of the wicked: but he blesseth the habitation of the just.

Pro 3:34 Surely he scorneth the   scorners: but he giveth grace unto the lowly.

Pro 3:35 The wise shall inherit glory: but shame shall be the promotion of fools.

5. Remember, Jesus has told us in the Gospel of Matthew; All will be known by their fruit; Good trees bring forth good fruit (*True Christians will be known by the fruit born out of their heart when truly good deeds are done, not for gain of themselves, but for the gain of lifting up the needy*), and Bad trees bring forth bad fruit *(these are those who might do good only with expectation of a reward or gain to themselves)*.

The Gospel of Matthew teaches us this in:
Matthew Chapter 7 verses 14 – 23;

Mat 7:14 Because strait is the gate, and narrow is the way, which leadeth unto life, and few there be that find it.
Mat 7:15 Beware of false prophets, which come to you in sheep's clothing, but inwardly they are ravening wolves.
Mat 7:16 Ye shall know them by their fruits. Do men gather grapes of thorns, or figs of thistles?
Mat 7:17 Even so every good tree bringeth forth good fruit; but a corrupt tree bringeth forth evil fruit.
Mat 7:18 A good tree cannot bring forth evil fruit, neither can a corrupt tree bring forth good fruit.
Mat 7:19 Every tree that bringeth not forth good fruit is hewn down, and cast into the fire.
Mat 7:20 Wherefore by their fruits ye shall know them.
Mat 7:21 Not every one that saith unto me, Lord, Lord, shall enter into the kingdom of heaven; but he that doeth the will of my Father which is in heaven.
Mat 7:22 Many will say to me in that day, Lord, Lord, have we not prophesied in thy name? and in thy name have cast out devils? and in thy name done many wonderful works?
Mat 7:23 And then will I profess unto them, I never knew you: depart from me, ye that work iniquity.

We must remember that when we do our best in all that we do, we are giving God Glory.
When we give thanks to and acknowledge that all we have has been given to us out of the blessings of God, we honor Him.

When we honor the Lord by helping the needy, (*Not in order to show off to others our work [such as the*

Pharisees]), but to sincerely to help them with a hand up, in order to possibly help them to get back on their feet, without expectation of reward at the moment, but in Heaven to lay at our Savior's feet, we again might be planting seeds for His Harvest, where in turn they might also help others because the look back at when someone helped them up, this is how the Spirit of the LORD may work through us, enabling Him to draw more lost, downtrodden, and hurting souls unto Himself.

So remember,

    The next time you feel that you are not hurting anyone if (who cares if I only do my job half, it isn't like I get paid very much to do it anyway) or (what does it matter if I slack off my studies, who cares if I don't graduate High School or College);

    Remember and think; (how many opportunities am I missing to spread the GOOD NEWS); there is light at the end of the tunnel for all that might hear it and accept it, that Jesus Christ paid our sin penalty by His death on that old rugged cross, and raising again after three days and now sits at the right hand of the Throne of the FATHER, as an Intermediary on our behalf Granting us the free gift of Eternal Life. We may be the closest thing that some may come to reading the Bible, When people look at you, can they see Jesus at first glance? Do they see in you a Warm and Bright Light that they would like to hear, learn more of, and receive? Or when others see you, do you just blend in with the rest of the world?

John E. Knopp Jr.

Chapter Four:
Study, Sharing, Helping others.

If you were given a unexpected quiz on Christianity and the Bible, how well would you fair?
What kind of Score would you receive?
Even on the most basic and famous Biblical Scriptures?

1. Who is GOD?
2. Who is Jesus?
3. How was the world formed?
4. How many days was the world created in?
5. What were the names of the first two people of creation?
6. Who was Noah? What did he do that was of importance?
7. Who was Moses? What did he do that was of importance?
8. Who was Abram? Why was his name changed to Abraham?

9. What significant test did GOD give to Abraham? What did he do?

10. Who was Isaac?

11. Who was Jacob? What to and why was his name changed?

12. Who was Joseph? What happened to him?

13. Who was Samuel?

14. Who was Saul? (Old Testament) (New Testament)

15. Who was David?

16. Who was Solomon?

17. Who was Jonah? What did God ask him to do? What happened to him?

Families should read, study, the Word of God. The Father should make it his concern to teach his family; in order for his family know why and how to know who God is, Who Jesus is and what He did on our behalf, and how to live a truly Godly lifestyle.

When you help someone in need, or share what you have to a stranger, (*as my Mother would say*) you never know when you may be entertaining Angels, or a Messenger of GOD!!!

We can only help others come to know Jesus by knowing Him ourselves. Can anyone teach something to someone else if they first do not learn it?

Remember, when families come together in prayer, Bible study, and make it a point to make family time, sharing true love with each other, and learn how to serve the Lord, giving thanks, worship, and giving back a portion of what He has allowed us to receive, learning to lean on Him in all things, your family will grow in the strength of true love, and Sharing will become second nature, bringing joy even in the worst of times.

God Loves you; He created you, and sent His Son (Jesus) to pay your penalties for your sin debt. All you have to do is accept Him, and follow Him.

Are you ready?

When we wake-up and realize; There is nothing that we can truly do of ourselves; it is GOD that allows kings and leaders to rise and fall, and it is when we are truly at our lowest, it is then that GOD our FATHER, and SAVIOUR works HIS best through us and brings glory unto HIMSELF.

When we make it a point to put **HIM** in the **Center** of our lives, putting **HIM** first, and we follow **HIS** Commands, Living them in our lifestyle, Teaching them to our Children and Grandchildren, that we will see that our lives are made **Successful by and through HIM**.

When we are Living for Jesus and Teaching others to do the same, helping to make Great HIS Harvest, we will find our Joy in this life to be in Abundance.

If we all would live by the Standards as taught in the Bible, I believe that we would see less people in poverty, we would have less time on our hands for mischief, and after a good day of hard work, play, or learning, we would all be able to sleep better at night.

I pray that the LORD may give HIS Mercy, Grace, and Blessings to all who might Study HIS WORD, Sharing it with Others, lifting up the weak and the lost, and living in HIS WORD, that we all might live a life that is Abundant in Joy, Love, Happiness, and Blessings that is of our FATHER's Will.

NOT the END as Jesus has not yet Returned, Are you and your family Ready?

A Guide to Having a Successful and Happy Home and Family Life

John E. Knopp Jr.

www.ingramcontent.com/pod-product-compliance
Lightning Source LLC
Chambersburg PA
CBHW052104110526
44591CB00013B/2351